OUR SENSES

How Smell Works

Sally Morgan

PowerKiDS
press.

New York

Published in 2011 by The Rosen Publishing Group Inc.
29 East 21st Street, New York, NY 10010

First Edition

Editor: Nicola Edwards
Designer: Robert Walster
Picture researcher: Shelley Noronha
Series consultant: Kate Ruttle
Design concept: Paul Cherrill

Library of Congress Cataloging-in-Publication Data

Morgan, Sally.
   How smell works / Sally Morgan. — 1st ed.
      p. cm. — (Our senses)
   Includes index.
   ISBN 978-1-61532-554-2 (library binding)
   ISBN 978-1-61532-561-0 (paperback)
   ISBN 978-1-61532-562-7 (6-pack)
   1. Smell—Juvenile literature. 2. Nose—Juvenile literature.
   I. Title.
   QP458.M67 2011
   612.8'6—dc22

5711   2009044490

Photographs:
Cover, 4 Blend Images/ImagePick; title page, 5 Tina Lorien/ istock;
2, 12 © Sean Justice/Corbis; 6 Ecoscene/Chinch Gryniewicz;
7 © Birgid Allig/zefa/Corbis; 8 © Adrian Muttitt/Alamy;
9 © Creasource/Corbis; Shutterstock/ ZQFotography;
11 Vasko Miokovic/istock; 12 © Sean Justice/Corbis;
13 Ryan McVay/Getty; 14 Code Red, George Hall/Getty;
15 Ecoscene/Robert Pickett; 16 Ecoscene/Bruan Cushing;
17 Ecoscene/Robert Pickett; 18 Ecoscene/ Satyendra
Tiwari; 19 David Tipling/ naturepl.com; 20 © Anna
Clopet/Corbis; 21 Billy Hustace/Getty; 22 Martyn f.
Chillmaid; 23l Christian Weibell/istock; 23r Roman
Pavlyuk/istock

Manufactured in China
CPSIA Compliance Information: Batch #WAS0102PK: For Further Information
contact Rosen Publishing, New York, New York at 1-800-237-9932

Web Sites

Due to the changing nature of Internet
links, PowerKids Press has developed
an online list of Web sites related to
the subject of this book. This site is
updated regularly. Please use this link
to access this list:
http://www.powerkidslinks.com/os/smell

Contents

Our Smelly World

Smell is one of the five senses. Our senses tell us things about the world around us.

Our five senses are hearing, sight, smell, taste, and touch.

We use our sense of smell when we cook food.

Some things, such as clean clothes and scented flowers, have a pleasant smell. Other things, such as rotting food and garbage on the street, smell horrible.

Some flowers give off a strong scent.

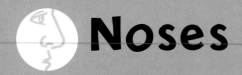 Noses

Noses vary in shape. There are long noses, short noses, wide noses, and turned-up noses! What shape is your nose?

How would you describe the shape of these noses?

You have a nose with two openings called nostrils. You smell by breathing in through your nostrils. Stand outside and sniff the air. What can you smell?

Words you can use to describe smells include: clean, fresh, musty, sharp, sweet, sour.

Imagine you are sniffing these towels. What might they smell like?

How Do We Smell?

Smells travel through the air to your nose. The smells tickle special detectors inside your nose. These send messages to your brain so that you can identify the smell.

We feel hungry when we smell food being cooked.

Perfume has a pleasant smell. When we spray perfume, tiny droplets of it float around in the air. The droplets travel through the air into the nose.

Food and Smell

Smell helps us to decide if food is good to eat. A lovely smell makes us want to eat something.

We can use our sense of smell to check if a pineapple is ripe.

A bad smell stops us from eating some foods. It is a warning that they will taste horrible and might make us sick.

Fresh bread smells sweet, but bread that smells sour and moldy is not safe to eat.

Milk that has spoiled smells bad.

Smell and Taste

Your senses of smell and taste work together. You sniff food before you put it in your mouth. As you chew your food, smells travel upward into the back of your nose.

These cupcakes smell good enough to eat!

When you have a cold, your nose gets blocked. You cannot breathe through your nose, so you cannot taste your food.

Can you taste food when you hold your nose?

Warning Smells

Some smells are warnings. The gas that we use for heating and cooking has a smell added to it. This means we can smell the gas if it escapes.

We smell smoke and flames before we see them.

Some animals release strong smells. Often, this is a warning to other animals to stay away.

If people or other animals come too close to a skunk, it sprays them with a revolting smelly liquid.

Some animals release smells to attract other animals.

Animal Noses

Animals have a sense of smell, too.
Many, such as horses, dogs, and cats,
use their noses for smelling.

The proboscis
monkey has
a very long
nose.

The word
proboscis
means
nose.

Some animals smell with other parts of their bodies. Snakes have nostrils, but they smell with their tongue.

This snake flicks out its tongue to smell its surroundings.

Expert Sniffers

Some people have a really good sense of smell. They may be able to tell the difference between as many as 10,000 different smells.

Perfume makers need an excellent sense of smell.

Many animals have a better sense of smell than people. Dogs have large nostrils and many smell detectors in their nose.

A sniffer dog at work.

Sniffer dogs are trained to find explosives and drugs by their smell.

Make a Smelly Pizza!

Choose some smelly pizza toppings, such as blue cheese, anchovies, olives, spicy sausage, smoked bacon, and onion.

Now build your pizza. First, spread the tomato paste over the base. Then add your toppings. Next, grate some mozzarella cheese on top.

Ask an adult to bake the pizza in an oven for you.

When the cooked pizza has cooled slightly, do a smell test. Do the cooked toppings smell different from before?

Finally, do a taste test!

You will need:
- a pizza base
- tomato paste
- mozzarella cheese
- a selection of smelly toppings

What's Your Favorite Smell?

Often, we link a smell with a memory. Have you ever visited a beach and smelled the sea? Perhaps you have visited a farm and remember the different animal smells.

Try to remember the smells of the different places you have visited. Can you describe the smells?

Glossary and Further Information

brain the control center of the body, found inside the head

detectors things that detect that something is there

expert knowing a lot about a subject, or having a special skill

nostrils openings in the nose

rotting decaying

scented having a smell

senses functions of the body through which we gather information about our surroundings

sniffer dogs dogs that are trained to find things such as drugs by their smell

Books

Animals And Their Senses: Animal Smell
by Kirsten Hall
(Weekly Reader Early Learning Library, 2005)

The Sense of Smell
by Ellen Weiss
(Children's Press, 2009)

World of Wonder: Smell
by Judy Wearing
(Weigl Publishers, 2009)

You Can't Taste Pickle With Your Ear
by Harriet Ziefert
(Blue Apple Books, 2006)

Index